THE UNEXPLAINED

BIGFOOT

BY PAUL THEISEN

BELLWETHER MEDIA · MINNEAPOLIS, MN

Are you ready to take it to the extreme?
Torque books thrust you into the action-packed world
of sports, vehicles, mystery, and adventure. These books
may include dirt, smoke, fire, and dangerous stunts.
WARNING : read at your own risk.

Library of Congress Cataloging-in-Publication Data

Theisen, Paul.
 Bigfoot / by Paul Theisen.
    p. cm. (Torque: The unexplained)
 Summary: "Engaging images accompany information about Bigfoot. The combination
of high-interest subject matter and light text is intended for students in grades 3 through
7"--Provided by publisher.
 Includes bibliographical references and index.
 ISBN 978-1-60014-498-1 (hardcover : alk. paper)
 1. Sasquatch--Juvenile literature. I. Title.
 QL89.2.S2T44 2010
 001.944--dc22   2010008474

This edition first published in 2011 by Bellwether Media, Inc.

Printed in the United States of America, North Mankato, MN.

120110   1179

CONTENTS

CHAPTER 1
A CREATURE IN THE WOODS ... 4

CHAPTER 2
WHAT IS BIGFOOT? 8

CHAPTER 3
SEARCHING FOR ANSWERS 16

GLOSSARY 22

TO LEARN MORE 23

INDEX 24

CHAPTER 1
A CREATURE IN THE WOODS

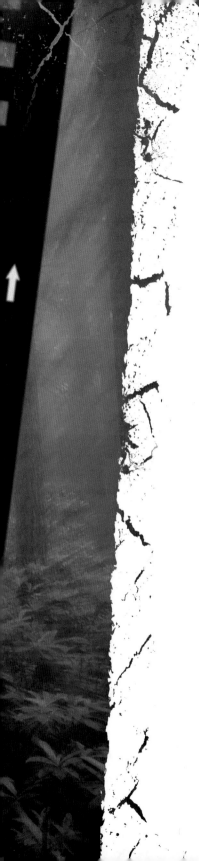

In October of 1967, Roger Patterson and Bob Gimlin were riding horses through California's Six Rivers National Forest. They were searching for the legendary creature called Bigfoot. Suddenly, Patterson's horse sensed something. The horse jerked back and threw Patterson off. A large, hairy creature was in the woods. It looked like an ape. Patterson grabbed his video camera.

Patterson pointed the camera toward the creature. He filmed the creature walking for a few seconds. Then it disappeared into the woods. The men did not see the creature again.

Patterson and Gimlin found footprints at the site where they saw Bigfoot. Molds of the prints measured almost 15 inches (38 centimeters) long.

BIG FEET

Patterson

Gimlin

News of the film spread quickly. Some people thought Patterson had proven that Bigfoot was real. **Skeptics** thought the film might be a **hoax**. There was no way to be sure. Bigfoot remained a mystery.

CHAPTER 2

WHAT IS BIGFOOT?

T ales of a large, wild, human-like creature are told all around the world. The most famous stories come from North America's Pacific Northwest. Some people there say Bigfoot lives deep in the forests of the region.

Pacific Northwest

North America

According to most reported sightings, Bigfoot is a **primate**. It is closely related to human beings and apes. Most witnesses describe a very large **biped**. Some have said it stands as tall as 10 feet (3 meters) and weighs at least 500 pounds (227 kilograms). It is covered in thick, reddish brown fur. It has long arms, big hands, and a small head.

primate

10 feet
(3 meters)

6 feet
(1.8 meters)

Most people who have come close to Bigfoot agree that it stinks. They say it smells like burnt rubber or manure.

PLUG YOUR NOSE

A few people believe that Bigfoot is **nocturnal**. They say it rarely comes out during the day. That could explain why the creature is so hard to find.

Bigfoot Names Around the World

Australia	Yowie
Brazil	Mapinguari
Canada	Sasquatch
China	Yeren
Japan	Hibagon
Mongolia	Almas
Scotland	Fear Liath More
Siberia (Russia)	Chuchunaa
Tibet	Yeti
United States	Bigfoot
Venezuela	Mono Grande
Vietnam	Batutut

BIGFOOT SIGHTINGS

Year	Place
1871	Mongolia
1924	Washington State
1941	Canada
1951	Mount Everest
1967	California
2000	Wisconsin
2000	Oregon
2007	Pennsylvania
2009	Oregon

Event

Explorer Nikolai Przewalski reports Bigfoot-like "wild men" living in Mongolia.

A group of miners claims to have been attacked by a group of ape-like creatures.

A mother and her children describe a Bigfoot that approached their home.

A group of climbers finds strange tracks in the snow, reportedly made by Bigfoot.

Roger Patterson and Bob Gimlin take their famous video of Bigfoot.

A delivery man spots a creature carrying a goat under its arm; he claims the creature is 8 feet (2.4 meters) tall.

Matthew Johnson sees and hears a strange, ape-like animal while hiking in the woods.

A hunter photographs a creature that looks like Bigfoot; skeptics call the creature a sick, skinny bear.

Hunters see two tall, dark-furred bipeds run across a road at speeds too fast for humans.

CHAPTER 3

SEARCHING FOR ANSWERS

hominid

T he debate over whether Bigfoot exists has gone on for more than 100 years. Some people insist Bigfoot is real. There are a few **theories** about what Bigfoot might be. Many people say it is a **hominid**. Some have suggested that Bigfoot could be a person who left **civilization** to live in the wild. Others think Bigfoot is a hoax, or reported sightings are of familiar animals like bears.

GIGANTO WHAT?

Some people think Bigfoot is a species called *Gigantopithecus*. Scientists believe this species of primate, which is related to modern humans, is extinct.

Gigantopithecus

Jeffrey Meldrum, a Bigfoot researcher, shows off what he claims is a plaster cast of a Bigfoot footprint.

TRACKING THE BEAST

BFRO keeps track of the number of reported Bigfoot sightings in the United States. The states with the most reported sightings are California, Oregon, and Washington.

The Bigfoot Field Researchers Organization (BFRO) formed in 1995 to collect **evidence** of Bigfoot. Researchers use many methods to look for proof. Some search for Bigfoot footprints. They make **plaster** casts of possible footprints when they find them. A few set up video cameras in remote areas and try to catch a glimpse of the creature. Others make sound recordings. They hope to capture the call of Bigfoot.

Will researchers ever find Bigfoot? Skeptics believe there's nothing out there to find. Others believe Bigfoot exists but stays far away from people. A handful of researchers believe it's only a matter of time before Bigfoot is found. They keep searching for the evidence that will show the world that Bigfoot is real. Do you think they'll ever solve the mystery?

GLOSSARY

biped—a creature that moves around on two legs

civilization—modern, advanced society

evidence—physical proof of something

hoax—an attempt to trick people into believing something

hominid—an early human

nocturnal—most active at night

plaster—a mixture of sand, water, and other materials that starts as a liquid and hardens into a solid; plaster is used to make casts, or impressions, of things such as footprints.

primate—a member of the order of mammals that includes people, apes, and monkeys

skeptics—people who do not believe in something

theories—ideas that try to explain why something exists or happens

TO LEARN MORE

AT THE LIBRARY

Cox, Greg. *Bigfoot*. New York, N.Y.: Rosen Publishing, 2002.

DeMolay, Jack. *Bigfoot: A North American Legend*. New York, N.Y.: PowerKids Press, 2007.

Townsend, John. *Bigfoot and Other Mysterious Creatures*. New York, N.Y.: Crabtree Publishing, 2009.

ON THE WEB

Learning more about Bigfoot is as easy as 1, 2, 3.

1. Go to www.factsurfer.com.

2. Enter "Bigfoot" into the search box.

3. Click the "Surf" button and you will see a list of related Web sites.

With factsurfer.com, finding more information

INDEX

1967, 5

1995, 19

ape, 5, 10

Bigfoot Field Researchers Organization (BFRO), 19

biped, 10

California, 5, 19

civilization, 16

evidence, 19, 21

extinction, 17

film, 5, 7

footprints, 6, 18, 19

Gigantopithecus, 17

Gimlin, Bob, 5, 6

height, 10, 11

hoax, 7, 16

hominid, 16

Meldrum, Jeffrey, 18

nocturnal, 13

North America, 9

Oregon, 19

Pacific Northwest, 9

Patterson, Roger, 5, 6, 7

plaster cast, 18, 19

primate, 10, 17

sightings, 10, 16, 19

Six Rivers National Forest, 5

skeptics, 7, 21

smell, 12

sound recordings, 19

theories, 16

video camera, 5, 19

Washington, 19

weight, 10

The images in this book are reproduced through the courtesy of: Jon Eppard, front cover, pp. 20-21; Topham/Fortean/The Image Works, p. 4; Fortean Picture Library, p. 6; Dale O'Dell/Alamy, pp. 7, 8-9; Juan Martinez, pp. 9 (small), 12-13, 14-15; Mike Price, p. 10 (small); Yuri Arcurs, pp. 10-11; E.G. Pors, p. 16; Denis, Finnin, American Museum of Natural History, p. 17; Jesse Harlan Alderman/AP Images, p. 18; John Marshall/AP Images, p. 19.